Presented to

Sue & Steve Wehrtor

From

_____

Date

7 - 1999

Once Upon A Romance

Compiled by
Heather Harpham Kopp

Harvest House Publishers
Eugene, Oregon

Once Upon a Romance

Copyright © 1997 Heather Harpham Kopp

Published by Harvest House Publishers

Eugene, Oregon 97402

Library of Congress Cataloging-in-Publication Data

Once upon a romance / (selected and introduced by) Heather Harpham Kopp.

   p. cm.

   ISBN 1-56507-660-5

   1. Love--Literary collections. 2. American literature.

3. English literature. I. Harpham, Heather.

PS509.L680536 1997

810.8'03543--dc21   97-2766

                                                  CIP

Design and production by Koechel Peterson & Associates, Minneapolis, Minnesota

Heather Harpham Kopp and Harvest House Publishers have made every effort to trace the ownership of all copyrighted poems and/or quotes and obtain permission for their use. In the event of any question arising from the use of a poem or quote, we regret any error made and will be pleased to make the necessary correction in future editions of this book.

Scriptures are from the Holy Bible, New International Version®. Copyright © 1973, 1978, 1984 by the International Bible Society. Used by permission of Zondervan Publishing House.

Printed in the United States of America

97 98 99 00 01 02 03 04 05 06 / BG / 10 9 8 7 6 5 4 3 2 1

For

Bill and Sheila Jensen

Contents

Once Upon a Time...

*I am certain of nothing but the holiness of the heart's affections
and the truth of imagination. . . .*

—John Keats

The awakening of love between a man and a woman is surely one of life's most sacred, glorious dramas. It's a story of tender truth that's been written about with endless imagination for centuries.

So what draws us to such stories again and again?

Certainly, it's because we *all* have a love story—what we once had, still have, or yet long for. When the brave suitor embraces his beloved at last, we feel our own longings embraced. When dreams turn bittersweet, or the cost of devotion runs high, we read our own soul's passionate journey on the page.

The stories celebrated here remind us that love is a delicious tangle of delight, discovery, and destiny. Through these words, begin to cherish your own, true love stories even more. And pursue a way of love that is beautiful, noble, and ends happily ever after.

A Heart First Stirs

*There's nothing half so
sweet in life as love's young dream.*

—Thomas Moore

Who will ever forget the first crush, the first kiss, the first time love was budding like a rose in your soul? The sun seemed brighter, the sky bluer. . . . A scented love note, a shy glance, or a certain caller's voice could stop the world from spinning.

First encounters with romance can be deliciously disorienting. To fall in love at first is to grow sick and well at the same time. It is to be hopelessly lost one moment and in the next, find home at last.

It is to begin one of life's sweetest journeys. . . .

Sweet Stranger

Seventeen
Booth Tarkington

William Sylvanus Baxter saw her while yet she was afar off. The thoroughfare was empty of all human life, at the time, save for those two; and she was upon the same side of the street that he was; thus it became inevitable that they should meet, face to face, for the first time in their lives.

He had perceived even in the distance, that she was unknown to him, a stranger, because he knew all the girls in this part of town who dressed as famously in the mode as that! And then, as the distance between them lessened, he saw that she was ravishingly pretty; far prettier, indeed, than any girl he knew. At least it seemed so, for it is, unfortunately, much easier for strangers to be beautiful.

His heart—his physical heart—began to do things the like of which, experienced by an elderly person, would have brought the doctor in haste. In addition, his complexion altered—he broke out in fiery patches. He suffered from breathlessness and from pressure on the diaphragm. He felt that his agitation was ruinous and must be perceptible at a distance of miles, not feet. And then, in the instant of panic that befell, when her dark-lashed eyelids slowly lifted, he had a flash of inspiration.

He opened his mouth somewhat, and as her eyes met his, full and startlingly, he placed three fingers across the orifice, and also offered a slight vocal proof that she had surprised him in the midst of a yawn.

For the fraction of a second, the deep blue spark in her eyes glowed brighter—gentle arrows of turquoise shot him through and through—and then her glance withdrew from the ineffable collision. . . .

Blonde Crush

The Adventures of Tom Sawyer
Mark Twain

As he was passing by the house where Jeff Thatcher lived, he saw a new girl in the garden—a lovely little blue-eyed creature with yellow hair, plaited into two long tails, white summer frock, and embroidered pantalets. The fresh-crowned hero fell without firing a shot. A certain Amy Lawrence vanished out of his head and left not even a memory of herself behind. He had thought he loved her to distraction, he had regarded his passion as adoration; and behold it was only a poor little evanescent partiality. He had been months winning her; she had confessed hardly a week ago; he had been the happiest and the proudest boy in the world only seven short days, and here in one instant of time she had gone out of his heart like a casual stranger whose visit is done.

He worshipped this new angel with furtive eye till he saw that she had discovered him; then he pretended he did not know she was present, and began to "show off" in all sorts of absurd boyish ways, in order to win her admiration. He kept up this grotesque foolishness for some time; but by and by, while he was in the midst of some dangerous gymnastic performances, he glanced aside and saw that the little girl was wending her way toward the house. Tom came up to the fence and leaned on it, grieving, and hoping she would tarry yet a while longer. She halted a moment on the steps and then moved toward the door. Tom heaved a great sigh as she put her foot on the threshold. But his face lit up, right away, for she tossed a pansy over the fence a moment before she disappeared.

A Swarm of Lads and a Little Rose

Little Men
Louisa May Alcott

Bess appealed

to the chivalrous

instinct in them

as something to

love, admire, and

protect with a

tender sort

of reverence.

Like a swarm of bees about a very sweet flower, the affectionate lads surrounded their pretty playmate, and kissed her till she looked like a little rose, not roughly, but so enthusiastically that nothing but the crown of her hat was visible for a moment. Then her father rescued her, and she drove away still smiling and waving her hands, while the boys sat on the fence screaming like a flock of guinea-fowls, "Come back! come back!" till she was out of sight.

They all missed her, and each dimly felt that he was better for having known a creature so lovely, delicate, and sweet; for little Bess appealed to the chivalrous instinct in them as something to love, admire, and protect with a tender sort of reverence. Many a man remembers some pretty child who has made a place in his heart and kept her memory alive by the simple magic of her innocence; these little men were just learning to feel this power, and to love its gentle influence, not ashamed to let the small hand lead them, nor to win their loyalty to womankind, even in the bud.

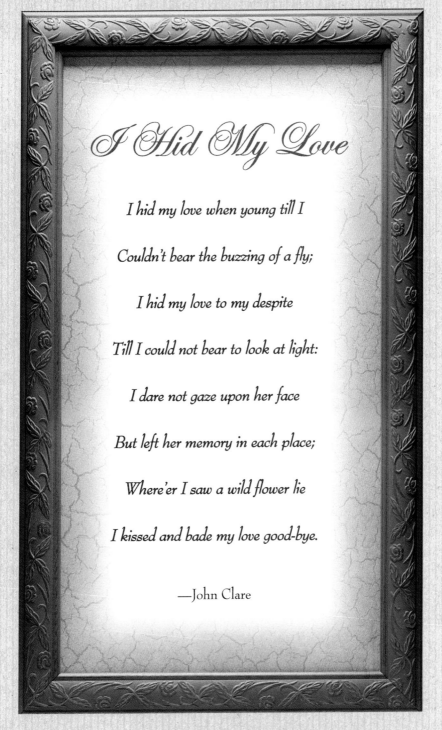

I Hid My Love

I hid my love when young till I

Couldn't bear the buzzing of a fly;

I hid my love to my despite

Till I could not bear to look at light:

I dare not gaze upon her face

But left her memory in each place;

Where'er I saw a wild flower lie

I kissed and bade my love good-bye.

—John Clare

Just One Look

The Able McLaughlins
Margaret Wilson

He tried hard enough, as he grew stronger, to shake off his depression. There were plenty of girls in the world whom he might marry, weren't there? The trouble was, he didn't like other girls. Still, he couldn't let merely one woman make him unhappy, could he? Not much! He used to be happy all the time, before he got to thinking about her so much. He would brace up, he vowed, and forget her.

The next Sunday he walked with his brothers to the church. The man of God read the Scriptures, and then at last came that welcomed long prayer, good for fifteen minutes at least.

Wully, sitting determinedly in a certain well-considered place in the pew, bowing his head devoutly and bending just a bit to one side, could watch Chirstie through his fingers, where she sat on the other side of the church. Her eyes were closed, but his did a week's duty. There was no doubt about it. She was getting thinner and thinner. It wasn't just his imagination. She was paler. She was unhappy. He had noticed that week by week. Surely she was not happy!

The minister was an indecent man, cutting that prayer short in so unceremonious a fashion. But after the sermon there would be another prayer, just a glimpse long. He had that to look forward to.

Finally the last prayer came. He turned his head, and there—oh, Chirstie was looking at him! With head bowed, but eyes wide open, she was looking at him! Hungrily, tenderly, pitifully, just as he wanted her to look. Their eyes met, and her face blossomed red. She turned her head hastily away. Let her turn away! Let her pray! He *knew*, now.

For some reason she didn't mean him to understand. But he had found out! It was all right. He could wait. He could wait any length of time, if only she would look at him again in that way! The congregation had risen, and had begun the Psalm. He would tell her, then and there, how glad he was, how he understood!

He lifted up his voice and sang, sang louder than anyone else.

You have stolen my heart

with one glance of your eyes.

—The Song of Songs

In the Kingdom of Love

Song of Years
Bess Streeter Aldrich

Suzanne was picking berries in the far end of the Martin property. She was also thinking of Wayne Lockwood. Suzanne thought she had never seen so good-looking a young man. Something made you like just everything about him, the way his wavy light hair went back from his forehead, his direct looking blue eyes, the way he held his head, the way his mouth pulled up at the corners when he smiled, that light-footed way of his walking. Even his strong brown hands pleased her.

Suzanne had a game of her very own which no one of the family knew anything about. She had a secret gift whereby she could live in either one of two worlds, just as she chose, and she scarcely knew which one she liked better. It was no trouble at all to change from one to the other, as easy, almost, as opening the wooden door between the main room and the lean-to.

. . . There were no sounds now in the sleepy warmth of the day excepting a few plaintive mourning doves' calls and the occasional plop of some water animal. And then suddenly she heard movement in the bushes as of light-footed walking, and her heart stood still with fright. Her body turned cold and she shook a little in the summer heat. Then Wayne Lockwood, gun in hand, came through the underbrush.

"Well, hello there," he was saying. "Where'd you come from? Are you lost?"

"Oh, no." Suzanne, relieved and happy, laughed aloud at that. "This place belongs to me."

She had never been one moment alone with him. The few times she had seen him the whole family had been around, as like as not plaguing her, too. For the first time she felt at ease in his presence.

"So this is yours, is it? Then I must be trespassing. Well, *Princess* Suzanne"—he swept off his cap, placed it across his breast, and bowed low in mock homage—"will you kindly allow me to cross your domain so that I can get to my castle on the other side of the Black Forest?"

Suzanne's eyes were wide with astonishment and she could not know how the playful words had lighted the candles that lay behind them. No one had ever said anything like that but her secret people. That was the way they talked. That was the way they acted. Her face grew pink with the excitement and embarrassment of it, and her voice trembled when she said shyly, "Yes, I guess I'll let you this once."

Long after he had gone on, turning around to laugh that he was walking here only by her permission, she remembered just how he looked and what he said.

It was going to be very, very easy after this to live in that magic world.

We are in love's land today;

Where shall we go?

Love, shall we start or stay,

Or sail or row?

There's many a wind and way

And never a May but May;

We are in love's hand today;

Where shall we go?

—Swinburne

Reluctant Swoon

Code of the West
Zane Grey

He climbed the pasture fence and walked across the level grassy field toward the bold dark ridge that towered almost mountain high. The loneliness and silence seemed to help him to think.

. . . Five, six hours before he had been Cal Thurman, who was now changed. It seemed a long time. A quarter of a day! Somewhere during that period he had fallen in love with this Georgiana May Stockwell. Pondering over the strange, undeniable circumstance, he decided he had done so on first sight.

. . .When, however, he thought of Georgiana—the newness and strangeness of her—the slim grace and dainty elegance—the pale sweet face, the golden curls, the dark blue eyes that could look as no others he had ever seen—when he remembered the alluring proximity of her and how audaciously she had intruded that fact upon him, then his reasoning went into eclipse. His heart was stormed.

What availed the faint cries of his intelligence? She was not the kind of a girl he wanted to love. He could not decide what she really was. Only it did not matter. Every remembrance of her actions submerged him deeper. He was frightened, distressed. But she would never find it out and surely he would soon get over it. Tomorrow, perhaps! Judging from the affairs of Tonto youths, this was not so terrible. Yet how humiliating! Love at first sight! It was a mixture of queer sensations. He grew conscious of inward excitement, a throbbing of heart, a pang in his breast, a vague longing to abandon thought and revel in the sweetness of dream, languor, thrill. Yet it was bitter, too.

. . .What had she meant by all she had said and done? Then her face seemed close to him again, a pale oval with its mysterious black holes for eyes, its tempting lips.

Thus Cal paced the pasture, a prey to all that constituted the torment and pain and ecstasy of dawning love in a true heart.

The Stuff of Fairy Tales

Cinderella
free translation by Marcia Brown

Now when the king's son learned that a grand
princess, whom no one knew at all, had just arrived at the
palace, he ran out to receive her. He offered her his hand as
she alighted from the coach and led her into the ballroom,
where all the company was assembled. Then—a deep silence
fell over the room, everyone stopped dancing, the violins
stopped playing, all eyes turned to the great beauty of this
mysterious one. Only a low murmur rippled over the
gathering, "Oh, how beautiful she is!"

The king himself, old as he was, could not take his
eyes off her and whispered in a low voice to the queen that it
had been a long time since he had seen anyone so charming
and beautiful.

The ladies were busy studying her headdress and her
gown in order to have some made just like them the next
day. If only they could find stuffs as fine and workmanship
as skillful!

The young prince conducted Cinderella to the seat
of greatest honor and then led her out on the floor to dance.
She danced with so much grace that people wondered at her
more than ever. A most splendid feast was served, but the
prince did not taste a mouthful, so intent was he in gazing
at Cinderella.

The Lover Pursues His Beloved

My lover spoke and said to me,
"Arise, my darling,
my beautiful one, and come with me.
See! The winter is past; the rains are over and gone.
Flowers appear on the earth;
the season of singing has come. . . ."

—The Song of Songs

Falling in love is easy, compared to what comes next. The smitten suitor must act, must choose to risk his heart—maybe his all—to win the affections of his beloved. He must prove his courage and worth, perhaps against rival suitors who might seem at first to have the upper hand.

So he pursues with flowers, songs, and poetry. And perhaps she woos him too—or demurely resists, even retreats. After all, coyness is half the pleasure in this delicate dance. Lovers must move quickly, but not too fast; show interest, without looking too eager. And lovers must always be ready to learn a new step in the timeless waltz.

It Was You, All Along

The Girl He Left Behind
Helen Beecher Long

His hand released her hand. But gently he drew her toward him, his arm behind her shoulder. Her form yielded hesitatingly to his urging.

"I cannot claim that patriotism brought me back for these few weeks that I may remain, Ethel," he went on in a voice that suddenly became strangely husky. "I wanted to see you—face to face."

There was an awkward pause. She felt his hand on her shoulder tremble.

"I can't understand why it is that I never saw you in just the same light that I have since I've been away. But you have been in my thoughts continually—the girl I left behind!"

"Oh, of course—the business—" she began flutteringly.

"No, it wasn't the business, Ethel. It was you!" he cried.

"Me?" Her breast began to heave and her face glowed. He bent low that he might catch her eyes.

"Yes, you! I guess I was asleep, but I'm awake now. We were so close day after day—and I was so wrapped up in business—that I didn't realize how much you really meant to me."

"Oh!" It was the faintest kind of an exclamation. She wanted to speak, but for once the "perfectly capable person" could not say a word. Her heart was pounding.

"But it came to me all of a sudden, while I was in the hospital and while that very fluttery Helen Fuller was trying to wait on me. Then I realized that you were the only girl in the world for me—the only one!"

Again there was a silence. But now she raised her eyes to meet his and they were full of glorious tenderness. He clutched her close to him.

"I love you—oh, how I love you!" he murmured. "How I love you!"

"Oh, Mr. Bar—"

"Ethel!"

"Frank, then."

She spoke his name with such sweetness that it almost overpowered him. It was as if she had suddenly lifted the veil and was letting him look into her very soul. He still held her close. Now he suddenly kissed her, once, twice and again.

"Thank God!" he said reverently. "Thank God!"

In her soul she also thanked God for His goodness in bringing this man to her. But she could not speak. She could only cling tightly to him—and for a long while he felt her heart beating close to his own.

Whatever our souls are made of,

his and mine are the same.

—Emily Brontë

An Agony Prolonged

Girl of the Limberlost
Gene Stratton Porter

The month which followed was a reproduction of the previous June. There were long moth hunts, days of specimen gathering, wonderful hours with great books, big dinners all of them helped to prepare, and perfect nights filled with music.

Everything was as it had been, with the difference that Phillip was now an avowed suitor. He missed no opportunity to advance himself in Elnora's graces. At the end of the month he was no nearer any sort of understanding with her than he had been at the beginning. He revelled in the privilege of loving her, but he got no response. Elnora believed in his love, yet she hesitated to accept him, because she could not forget Edith Carr.

One afternoon early in July, Phillip came across the fields, through the Comstock woods, and entered the garden. He inquired for Elnora at the back door and was told that she was reading under the willow. He went around the west end of the cabin to her. She sat on a rustic bench they had made and placed beneath a dropping branch. Phillip had not seen her before in the dress she was wearing. It was clinging mull of pale green, trimmed with narrow ruffles and touched with knots of black velvet; a simple dress, but vastly becoming. Every tint of her bright hair, her luminous eyes, her red lips, and her rose-flushed face, neck, and arms grew a little more vivid with the delicate green setting.

Phillip stopped short. She was so near, so temptingly sweet, he lost control. He went to her with a half-smothered cry after that first long look, dropped on one knee beside her and reached an arm behind her to the bench back, so that he was very near. He caught her hands.

"Elnora!" he cried tensely, "end it now! Say this strain is over. I pledge you that you will be happy. You don't know! If you would say the word, you would awake to new life and great joy! Won't you promise me now, Elnora?"

The girl sat staring into the west wood, while strong in her eyes was her father's look of seeing something invisible to others. Phillip's arm slipped from the bench around her. His fingers closed firmly over hers, his face came very near.

"Elnora," he pleaded, "you know me well enough. You have had time in plenty. End it now. Say you will be mine!"

He gathered her closer, pressing his face against hers, his breath on her cheek.

"Can't you quite promise yet, my girl of the Limberlost?"

Love cannot be wasted.

It makes no difference where

it is bestowed, it always

brings in big returns.

—Anonymous

'Twas a Dream

Love Is Eternal
Irving Stone

She organized the materials in her mind and gave Abraham Lincoln an analysis of what she deduced locally and from the national press. He watched her with wide glowing eyes, now knowing that she had been steeped in just such clinical analysis at her father's dinner table.

When she stopped, he leaned across the space between them and gripped her shoulders.

"Molly, you are the most beautiful talker I've ever known. It's like pages read aloud from a book. If only I could talk that way when I'm up before crowds."

"Abraham, you came from a lonely background: the log cabin in the woods with the nearest neighbor miles away, the days spent solitary in the forest with your ax, with no one to talk to but yourself and the trees. I come from a highly convivial background where there were always many people around: twenty in a house, thirty in a classroom; fifty at a cotillion . . ." she chuckled, then added, "all talking at once."

He shook his head soberly.

"Molly, why is it you're the only young lady I feel comfortable with? Only one I ever have, for that matter."

"Perhaps it's because we're friends."

He peered at her for a moment. The room was still, the world locked out.

"It's more than that," he said; "but I know so little of what lies beyond friendship. . . ."

Then again their lips were sealed, as tightly and as mysteriously as they had been on the front porch in June before they had gone their separate ways. She could not think, not while Abraham had his arms crushing her to him, but she knew what she felt: that this was good, and right, and forever.

Slowly, reluctantly he unlocked his lips from hers, eased the crush of his embrace, moved back slightly though without releasing her, and looked at her with glazed, awe-filled eyes.

"Is that . . . what I meant . . . we're in love?"

[*The next day*]

. . . She jumped out of bed, gaily humming the words of "It Was a Dream, 'Twas a Dream," and sat in her nightgown before the mirror. She thought, I'm prettier now than I've ever been in my life. My eyes seem to be larger, my skin is clear and glowing, my hair is alive, easy to do things with. But I must stop using that scented oil on my brush: it's darkening my hair too much. Abraham may like it lighter. I must ask him.

She slipped into a dressing gown and went down to breakfast and a new world.

Progress by Moonlight

Katrine
Elinor McCartney Lane

In a thin white gown, low in the neck, with a kerchief of filmy lace knotted in front, sleeves that fell away at the elbow, with faint, pink roses at her breast, her black hair turned high in a curly knot, she stood in the old rose-garden when he came.

He wore a light overcoat over his evening dress, and stood hatless by the boxwood arch looking across at her. "Katrine," he said, "little Katrine, I have come back to you. . . ."

. . . She seemed to him so perfect, such an utterly desirable being, as she sat with roses in her hand and the moonlight shining on her flower-like face.

Neither noted the silence which fell between them, a silence which spoke more than language could have done, for language had become, between them, an unnecessary thing.

. . . It seemed as though they were alone together in the world. In the moonlit gloom under the pine they stood, near, nearer, and at length he put his arm around her gently, not drawing her toward him, only letting it lie around her waist, as though they had a right to be there, heart to heart, in the stillness of the night. Standing thus, he felt her tremble, noted her quickened breath, and the rise and fall of her shoulders.

Although they could not see each other in the gloom, she knew his lips sought hers. By an indefinable instinct she turned from him twice before their lips met. They kissed each other again before he drew her down beside him on the garden bench in the flower-scented dusk.

"You care?" she asked, in a whisper, her breath on his cheek.

"More than I thought I could care for anything in life," he answered.

Starlit Proposal

The Happy Golden Years
Laura Ingalls Wilder

"I was wondering . . ." Almanzo paused. Then he picked up Laura's hand that shone white in the starlight, and the sun-browned hand closed gently over it. He had never done that before. "Your hand is so small," he said. Another pause. Then quickly, "I was wondering if you would like an engagement ring."

"That would depend on who offered it to me," Laura told him.

"If I should?" Almanzo asked.

"Then it would depend on the ring," Laura answered, and drew her hand away.

It was later than usual when Almanzo came next Sunday.

"Sorry to be so late," he said, when Laura was settled in the buggy and they were driving away.

"We can take a shorter drive," Laura answered.

"But we want to go to Lake Henry. This is about our last chance for wild grapes, now they are frosted," Almanzo told her.

It was a sunny afternoon, warm for the time of year. On either side of the narrow road between the twin lakes, ripened wild grapes were hanging from their vines in the trees. Almanzo drove slowly, and reaching from the buggy he and Laura picked the clusters of grapes. They ate of their tangy sweetness and heard the little waves lapping on the shore.

As they drove home the sun went down in a flaming western sky. Twilight settled over the prairie, and the evening wind blew softly through the buggy.

Then driving with one hand, with the other Almanzo lifted Laura's, and she felt something cool slip over her first finger while he reminded her, "You said it would depend on the ring. How do you like this one?"

Laura held her hand up to the first light of the new moon. The gold of the ring and its flat oval set shone in the faint moon radiance. Three small stones set in the golden oval glimmered.

"The set is a garnet, with a pearl on each side," Almanzo told her.

"It is a beautiful ring," Laura said. "I think . . . I would like to have it."

"Then leave it on. It is yours and next summer I will build a little house in the grove on the tree claim. It will have to be a little house. Do you mind?"

"I have always lived in little houses. I like them," Laura answered.

Love is a desire of the

whole being to be united to some other being.

—Samuel Taylor Coleridge

Oh, the Baffling
Mysteries of Love!

But love is blind, and lovers cannot see
the pretty follies that themselves commit.

—Shakespeare

As lovers stumble toward love, inevitably hearts collide. One moment, both are lost in a delicious dream of love, and in the next—one has cast eternal bliss into doubt.

But something good can be made of these poignant mysteries. Such moments offer an opportunity for blessed insight, a change of heart, a humbled affection. And when born with grace and courage, the baffling trials of courtship prove that love can conquer all.

Hear My Heart

A Daughter of the South
George Cary Eggleston

Human nature is perhaps the queerest product of creation. . . . It is never consistent with itself. It is scarcely too much to say that it is never quite candid and truthful even in its dealings with itself.

When High Marvin, in his note, said to Gabrielle Latour, "Pray do not trouble yourself to send an answer," he probably meant it in a way. At least he meant that she should not feel under any obligation to send an answer. Yet all that day until the time came for him to board a late afternoon train for Chicago, he found himself waiting for an answer and uneasily wondering why no answer came.

Gabrielle in her turn was equally perplexed. She, with her absolute sincerity of mind, accepted the young man's words as meaning all that was said in them and perhaps a trifle more. "He is a very busy man of affairs," she reflected. "He is willing, in his kindly, almost fatherly way, to give up his early mornings to me, or rather, he likes to ride in the early morning, and he invites me to go with him because he thinks I enjoy it, as I certainly do. But he doesn't want to be bothered with notes from me, and so when he sends me all those delightful magazines, and politely writes a note to accompany them, he forbids me to say 'thank you.' Never mind, I'll say it when we meet again, and I'll say it in such a way that he shall know how truly I mean it."

Thus are cross-purposes set going in this whimsical world of ours. . . .

A man cannot take back

his heart after he has given it,

even though a woman does scorn it. . . .

—L. T. Meade

I do love nothing in

the world so well as you:

is not that strange?

—Shakespeare, *Much Ado About Nothing*

A Spark Misfired

The Tinder Box
Maria Thompson Davies

His dangerous eyes smoldered back at me for a long minute before he answered me:

"Men don't break women's hearts, Evelina."

"I think you are right," I answered slowly, "they do just wring and distort them and deform them for life. But I intend to see that Nell's has no such torturous operation performed on it if I can appeal to you to convince her."

"When you argue with Nell be sure and don't tell her just exactly the things *you* have done to *me* all this summer through, Evelina," he answered coolly.

"What do you mean?" I demanded, positively cold with a kind of astonished fear. . . .

". . . You have made yourself everything for me that is responsive and desirable and beautiful and worthy and have put me back every time I have reached out to grasp you. You don't want me, you don't want to marry me at all, you just want—excitement. You are as cold as ice that grinds and generates fire. Very well, you don't have to take me—and I'll get what I can from Nell— and others."

"Oh, Polk, how could you have misunderstood me like this?" I moaned from the depths of an almost broken heart. But as I moaned I understood—I understood!

I'm doing it all wrong! I had the most beautiful human love for him in my heart and he thought it was all dastardly, cold coquetting. An awful spark has been struck out of the flint. I'm not worthy to experiment with this dreadful man-and-woman question.

When first we met we did not guess

That Love would prove so hard a master;

Of more than common friendliness

When first we met we did not guess—

Who could foretell this sore distress—

This irresistible disaster

When first we met?

We did not guess

That love would prove so hard a master.

—Robert Bridges

She Thinks . . .

The Angel stood between them.

. . . McLean's arms dropped helplessly.

"You don't understand," he reiterated patiently. "It isn't the love of a friend, or a comrade, or a sister, that Freckles wants from you; it is the love of a sweetheart. And if to save the life he has offered for you, you are thinking of being generous and impulsive enough to sacrifice your future—in the absence of your father, it will become my plain duty, as the protector in whose hands he has placed you, to prevent such rashness. The very words you speak, and the manner in which you say them, prove that you are a mere child, and have not dreamed what love is."

Then the Angel grew splendid. A rosy flush swept the pallor of fear from her face. Her big eyes widened and dilated with intense lights. She seemed to leap to the height and the dignity of superb womanhood before their wondering gaze.

"I never have had to dream of love," she said proudly. "I never have known anything else, in all my life, but to love everyone and to have everyone love me. And there never has been anyone so dear as Freckles. If you will remember, we have been through a good deal together. I do love Freckles, just as I say I do.

"I don't know anything about the love of sweethearts, but I love him with all the love in my heart, and I think that will satisfy him. . . ."

He Thinks . . .

The Angel caught Freckles' hand and carried it to her breast.

"Freckles!" she wailed in terror, "Freckles! It is a mistake? Is it that you don't want me?"

Freckles' head rolled on in wordless suffering.

"Wait a bit, Angel?" he panted at last. "Be giving me a little time!"

The Angel arose with controlled features. She bathed his face, straightened his hair, and held water to his lips. It seemed a long time before he reached toward her. Instantly she knelt again, carried his hand to her breast, and leaned her cheek upon it.

"Tell me, Freckles," she whispered softly.

"If I can," said Freckles in agony. "It's just this. Angels are from above. Outcasts are from below. You've a sound body and you're beautifulest of all. You have everything that loving, careful raising and money can give you. I have so much less than nothing that I don't suppose I had any right to be born. It's a sure thing— nobody wanted me afterward, so of course, they didn't before. Some of them should have been telling you long ago."

"If that's all you have to say, Freckles, I've known that quite a while," said the Angel stoutly. "Mr. McLean told my father, and he told me. That only makes me love you more, to pay for all you've missed."

Freckles
Gene Stratton Porter

53

Mysterious Seeds of Love

Poor Dear Theodora
Florence Irwin

It would have been enough that Theodora did not love the man she had promised to marry, but it was as nothing compared with the flood of certainty that at last surged through her heart that she did love another man—and a man, at that, who had never even mentioned love nor marriage to her, and who was himself engaged to another woman.

Theodora knew now what had been the nature of that vague and lovely thing that had entered her heart a year ago—it had been the first tender shoot of the exquisite plant called Love. Its fragrance had permeated her days, making the past negligible, the present rose-hued, and the future golden-bright. And then, before she had as much as grasped the meaning of this new feel of life, along had come the tempest—uprooting her little plant and leaving it to wither.

It had been the haunting memory that there existed such things as the plant and its wonderful perfume, that had made Theodora first fear to engage herself to Gerald. All through her courtship with him, her heart had beat so sanely, her pulses had lain so quiet, her poise had been so normal. There had been none of that foolish certainty that *something* was about to glorify life, and that nothing really mattered, except that one was alive and young and not too hideously unattractive.

There had never existed that wonderful feeling that right around the next corner one would suddenly catch up with perpetual bliss. An experienced woman would instantly have recognized the symptoms that had merely made Theodora wonder throbbingly through the past two winters; a cynical woman would have said to herself, "Here's another swoon. Now I shall be restless and unhappy till it's over"; a romantic woman would have thrilled to the thought, "At last, true love has found me!" Poor dear Theodora, being neither experienced, nor cynical, nor especially romantic, had no clue to her mystery.

A Heady Feeling

Gone With the Wind
Margaret Mitchell

Frank came to call every night, for the
atmosphere of Pitty's house was pleasant and soothing.
Mammy's smile at the front door was the smile reserved
for quality folks, Pitty served him coffee and fluttered
about him and Scarlett hung on his every utterance.
Sometimes in the afternoons he took Scarlett riding with
him in his buggy when he went out on business. These
rides were merry affairs because she asked so many foolish
questions—"just like a woman," he told himself
approvingly. He couldn't help laughing at her ignorance
about business matters and she laughed too, saying: "Well,
of course, you can't expect a silly little woman like me to
understand men's affairs."

She made him feel, for the first time in his
old-maidish life, that he was a strong upstanding man
fashioned by God in a nobler mold than other men,
fashioned to protect silly helpless women.

When, at last, they stood together to be married,
her confiding little hand in his and her downcast lashes
throwing thick black crescents on her pink cheeks, he still
did not know how it all came about. He only knew he had
done something romantic and exciting for the first time
in his life. He had swept this lovely creature off her feet
and into his strong arms.

Love Resisted

Time of Roses
L. T. Meade

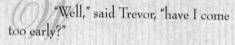

"I won't ask

you too

much; only

tell me,

sweetest,

with your

own lips

that you

love me."

"Well," said Trevor, "have I come too early?"

"Oh, no," said Florence, "it is past eleven," and she looked listlessly at the clock.

He tried to take her hand. She put it immediately behind her.

Trevor took out of his pocket a copy of the *General Review*. He opened it at the page where Florence's article appeared. He then also produced from his pocket-book a tiny slip of paper, a torn slip, on which, in Bertha Keys's handwriting, was the identical sentence which had attracted so much attention in the *Review*.

. . . "You read what was not meant for you to read!" said Florence, her eyes flashing.

Trevor gave her a steady glance.

"I admit that I read a sentence—the sentence I have just shown you. I will frankly tell you that I was surprised by it; I was puzzled by a resemblance between the style of the story and the style of the sentence. I put the torn sheet of paper into my pocket-book. I don't exactly know why I did it at the time, but I felt desperate. I was taking a great interest in you. It seemed to me that if you did wrong I was doing wrong myself. It seemed to me that if by chance your soul was smirched, or made unhappy, or blackened, or any of its loftiness and its god-like quality removed, my own soul was smirched, too, my own nature lowered.

"But I thought no special harm of you, although I was troubled; and that night I learned for the first time that I was interested in you because I loved you, because you were the first of all women to me, and I—"

"Oh, don't," said Florence, "don't say more." She turned away from him, flung herself on the sofa, and sobbed as if her heart would break.

Trevor stood near for a little, in much bewilderment. Presently she raised her eyes. He sat down on the sofa by her.

"Why don't you tell me everything, Florence?" he said, with great tenderness in his tone.

"I cannot: it is too late. Think what you like of me! Suspect me as you will! I do not think you would voluntarily injure me. I cannot give you my confidence, for I—"

"Yes, dear, yes; don't tremble so. Poor little girl, you will be better afterwards. I won't ask you too much; only tell me, sweetest, with your own lips that you love me."

"I am not sweet, I am not dear, I am not darling. I am a bad girl, bad in every way," said Florence. "Think of me as you like. I dare not be near you: I dare not speak to you. . . . I have accepted the part that is not good, and you must forget me."

When Will Love Come?

The Broken Wedding Ring
Charlotte Braeme

Some of the offers Miss Hatton received were dazzling ones. "Love!" said the duchess. "It will come with marriage."

"Not the love I want," she replied; "That must come before. I want a romance in my life."

"It is the way with those dark-eyed girls," said the duchess. "What a pity it is!"

. . . "You will marry some time, Leah," she said, with the resignation of despair.

"It is possible," she replied, smiling; "but it is more probable that I shall never marry at all."

"Should you mind telling me why?" asked the duchess, in tones of mock resignation.

"I will tell you, Duchess; but you will be angry with me. I want some one to love me more than life itself—some one to be devoted to me, to give me all his thoughts, his whole life. . . . I want his heart to be one with mine, his soul to be the other half of my soul. I want perfect love and I want a perfect lover. I have my ideal love, and no other will do; I have my ideal lover, and I shall wait for him."

Vowing
Eternal Love

As fair thou art, my bonnie lass,

So deep in love am I:

And I will love thee still, my dear,

Till a' the seas gang dry.

—Robert Burns

Courting, and the progress of love, may pass quickly or slowly. Many a smitten maiden has wondered: Is her beau's love just a fancy—or forever? But finally that sweetest of days comes, when her lover is moved to declare his intentions and undying devotion.

Sometimes a lover's confession may come as a shock to her—or even a revelation to himself. Or, both partners might rush to tell all in a mutual outburst of passion. No matter how carefully planned a proposal or proclamation of love, it feels like a wild surprise, a glorious risk one should have taken long ago.

With a Lad's Whole Heart

A Girl of the People
L. T. Meade

Will's figure no longer looked so slight and boyish; he held himself up very erect, and the breeze tossed back his thick dark curly hair, and the moonlight shone into his honest blue eyes, as they looked straight at the trembling, troubled, excited girl.

"You know as I'm your true love; and I'll wed you, come what may, " said Will Scarlett. "There—I stayed away from the bonny waves on purpose. Look at me, Bet, I'm the lad as has given his whole heart to you. . . ."

". . , I never thought as we was made for one another," she said, in a timid undertone.

"Then you knowed very little, Bet, if you didn't find that out. Away on the sea, haven't I dreamt of you, and seen your face near mine, when the waves was rough, and we thought we'd be in Davy Jones' locker by the morning? And sometimes, Bet, when I'd be tempted to do as other fellows, and take to bad ways, your face 'ud come before me, and somehow I couldn't. I always knew when I was out on the waves that you was to be my lawful wedded wife one day. . . .

". . . See, Bet, the moon's shining on us, and there's a beautiful salt taste of the sea on our lips, and there's all the love that I can give you shining out of my eyes this minute. You make me a promise, Bet, dear—one that will undo that base one you once vowed to yourself. Forget that promise—what were cruel and wicked, and a shame, when it came atween you and me. Here, make another now, Bet—one of your own as never go broke."

"What shall I say, Will? I'm troubled sore, and yet I'm comforted beyond words to say; and you ha' done it! Will, dear Will. What promise shall I make as I'll be true and binding on me forever?"

"Say this, Bet: 'I give myself to you, Will Scarlett, and I'll be your wedded wife as soon as ever parson can be found to tie us together. So help me, God Almighty.'"

Bet said the words without faltering, and as she did so a curious and wonderful thing happened to her—when she found her love, and believed in him, and gave herself up to him utterly, she also ceased to doubt that there was a God. He was there—He was good; He was blessing her. She had only twopence in her pocket, and her worldly career seemed a short hour ago utterly destroyed and done for; but now no girl in Liverpool could feel richer than she did.

Place me like a seal over your heart, like a seal on your arm;
for love is as strong as death, its jealousy unyielding as the grave.
It burns like blazing fire, like a mighty flame.
Many waters cannot quench love; rivers cannot wash it away.

—Song of Solomon

A Soul Set Free

Miss Petticoats
Dwight Tilton

"...I only know that I cannot forget, I cannot forgive."

"I admit your great wrongs. I frame no excuse for this man's brutality. It is for you I plead. Forgiveness is the greatest of the virtues, for it is the most difficult to practice. It is the most noble, for it is the most ennobling."

"My wrongs—their wrongs. You forget them!" she cried with an intensity that touched him deeply.

"No," he replied gently, "nor did He whose forgiveness is the beacon to us all, forget. He remembered, but He forgave."

"He was not mortal," she whispered. Then she looked him full in the eyes and added: "You, yourself, could not forgive."

"Couldn't I?" he asked with a sad smile. "I have forgiven. It was a great burden that sorely tried me, but I forgave him years ago."

"Hamilton?"

"Yes."

"What had you to forgive?" she queried, her eyes filled with questioning.

"The greatest thing he could have done to injure me," he answered gravely.

"To injure you? How could he injure you?"

"By injuring you," he said gently.

"By injuring me? I—don't understand."

"Yes, Agatha, by injuring you." He spoke rapidly now, and with a vehemence she had never before heard from his lips. "Yes, for I loved you, loved you then as I—as I love you now."

"You—love—me?"

She stood before him in adorable wonderment, her head bent forward toward his own, her lips parted and her eyes filled with a soft radiance.

His long repressed ardor burst forth in a torrent of tender words, a storm of passionate phrases that would not be denied. Never had he pleaded for a soul more eloquently than for the cause of his own manly heart, nor ever had he a more entranced listener. . . .

. . . With Agatha's love came implicit faith, and she relied upon Harding's counsel. . . . It was not that her scheme of vengeance had yielded to her now-found happiness; that would have been merely the exchange of one passion for another. No, she knew that there had been a new dawn, and that her love was but one of its radiant beams. Her soul . . . had been awakened to life and beauty. . . .

My love has placed her little hand

With noble faith in mine,

And vowed that wedlock's sacred band

Our natures shall entwine.

My love has sworn, with sealing kiss,

With me to live—to die;

I have at last my nameless bliss:

As I love—loved am I!

—Charlotte Brontë

The Home of Love

Barriers Burned Away
E. P. Roe

... He turned his face away, that she might not see the evidences of the bitter struggle within,—the severest he had ever known; but at last he spoke in the firm and quiet voice of victory.

... "Yes, Miss Ludolph," he said, "my silence is the part of true friendship,—truer than you can ever know. May Heaven's richest blessings go with you to your own land, and follow you through a long, happy life."

"My own land? This is my own land."

"Do you not intend to go abroad at once, and enter upon your ancestral estates as the Baroness Ludolph?"

"Not if I can earn a livelihood in Chicago," she answered, most firmly. "Mr. Fleet, all that nonsense has perished as utterly as this my former home. Mr. Fleet, you see before you a simple American girl. I claim and wish to be known in no other character. If nothing remains of my father's fortune I shall teach either music or painting—"

"O Christine!" he interrupted, "forgive me for speaking to you under the circumstances, but indeed I cannot help it. Is there hope for me?"

She looked at him so earnestly as to remind him of her strange, steady gaze when before he pleaded for her love near that same spot, but her hand trembled in his like a fluttering, frightened bird. In a low, eager tone she said, "And can you still truly love me after all the shameful past?"

"When have I ceased to love you?"

With a little cry of ecstasy, like the note of joy that a weary bird might utter as it flew to its mate, she put her arm around his neck, buried her face on his shoulder, and said, "No hope for you, Dennis, but perfect certainty, for now every barrier is burned away!"

What matter if the home before them was a deserted ruin? Love was joining hands that would build a fairer and better one, filled with that which alone makes a home—love.

What if all around them were only dreary ruins, where the night wind was sighing mournfully? Love had transformed that desert place into the paradise of God; and, if such is its power in the wastes of earthly desolation, what will be its might amid the perfect scenes of Heaven?

On the Face of Love

Jane Eyre
Charlotte Brontë

"Come to my side, Jane, and let us explain and understand one another."

"I will never again come to your side: I am torn away now, and cannot return."

"But, Jane, I summon you as my wife: it is you only I intend to marry."

I was silent: I thought he mocked me.

. . . "You—you strange—you almost unearthly thing!—I love as my own flesh. You—poor and obscure, and small and plain as you are—I entreat to accept me as a husband."

"What, me!" I ejaculated: beginning in his earnestness— and especially in his incivility—to credit his sincerity: "me who have not a friend in the world but you—if you are my friend: not a shilling but what you have given me?"

"You, Jane. I must have you for my own—entirely my own. Will you be mine? Say yes, quickly."

"Mr. Rochester, let me look at your face: turn to the moonlight."

"Why?"

"Because I want to read your countenance; turn!"

"There: you will find it scarcely more legible than a crumpled, scratched page. Read on: only make haste, for I suffer."

His face was very much agitated and very much flushed, and there were strong workings in the features, and strange gleams in the eyes.

"Oh, Jane, you torture me?" he exclaimed. "With that searching and yet faithful and generous look, you torture me!"

"How can I do that? If you are true and your offer real, my only feelings to you must be gratitude and devotion—they cannot torture."

"Gratitude!" he ejaculated: and added wildly—"Jane, accept me quickly. Say, 'Edward—give me my name—Edward—I will marry you.'"

"Are you in earnest?—Do you truly love me?—Do you sincerely wish me to be your wife?"

"I do; and if an oath is necessary to satisfy you, I swear it."

"Then, sir, I will marry you."

"... Come to me—come to me entirely now," said he: and added, in his deepest tone, speaking in my ear as his cheek was laid on mine, "Make my happiness—I will make yours."

An Imp's Love Letters

My Lady Caprice
Jeffery Farnol

The hole in the trunk needed little searching for. I remembered it well enough, and thrusting in my hand, drew out a folded paper. Holding this close to my eyes, I managed with no little difficulty to decipher this message:

> Don't go unkel dick bekors Auntie lisbeth wants you and i want you to. I heard her say so to herself in the libree and she was crying to, and didn't see me there but i was. And she said O Dick i want you so, out loud bekors she didn't no I was there. And i no she was crying bekors i saw the tiers. And this is true on my onner so help me sam.
>
> Sined,
> Your true frend and Knight,
> REGINALD AUGUSTUS

A revulsion of feeling swept over me as I read. Ah! if only I could believe she had said such words—my beautiful, proud Lisbeth.

Alas! dear Imp, how was it possible to believe you? And because I knew it could not possibly be true, and because I would have given my life to know that it *was* true, I began to read the note all over again.

Suddenly I started and looked round; surely that was a sob! But the moon's level rays served only to show the utter loneliness about me. It was imagination, of course, and yet it had sounded very real.

. . . Once again the sound came to me, low and restrained, but a sob unmistakably.

On the other side of the giant tree I beheld a figure half sitting, half lying. The shadow was deep here, but as I stooped the kindly moon sent down a shaft of silver light, and I saw a lovely, startled face, with great, tear-dimmed eyes.

"Lisbeth!" I exclaimed; then prompted by a sudden thought, I glanced around.

"I am alone," she said, interpreting my thought aright.

"But—here—and—and at such an hour!" I stammered foolishly. She seemed to be upon her feet in one movement, fronting me with flashing eyes.

"I came to look for the Imp. I found this on his pillow. Perhaps you will explain?" and she handed me a crumpled paper, and I read:

> Dear Auntie Lisbath: Unkel dick is going away bekors he is in luv with you and you are angry with the Blarsted oke, where I hid yore stokkings if you want to kiss me and be kind to me again, come to me bekors I want somebboddie to be nice to me now he is gone.

> yore luving sorry Imp.

> P.S. He said he would like to hand himself in his sword-belt to the arm of yonder tree and hurl himself from yon topmost pinnakel, so I no he is in luv with you.

"Oh, blessed Imp!"

"And now where is he?" she demanded.

"Lisbeth, I don't know."

"You don't know! Then why are you here?"

For answer I held out the letter I had found, and watched while she read the words I could not believe.

Her hat was off, and the moon made wonderful lights in the coils of her black hair. . . . Now as she finished reading she turned suddenly away, yet not before I had seen the tell-tale colour glowing in her cheeks—a slow wave which surged over her from brow to chin, and chin to the round, white column of her throat.

. . . "Lisbeth, is it true?"

She stood with her face averted, twisting the letter in her fingers.

"Lisbeth!" I said, and took a step nearer. Still she did not speak, but her hands came out to me with a swift, passionate gesture, and her eyes looked into mine; and surely none were ever more sweet, with the new shyness in their depths and the tears glistening on their lashes.

And in that moment Doubt and Fear were swallowed up in a great joy, and I forgot all things save that Lisbeth was before me and that I loved her.

His Tender Heart

The Book of Ruth

Now Naomi had an in-law in Bethlehem who was a very wealthy man. His name was Boaz.

One day Ruth said to Naomi, "Perhaps I can go out into the fields of some kind man to glean the free grain behind his reapers."

And Naomi said, "All right, dear daughter. Go ahead."

So she did. And as it happened, the field where she found herself belonged to Boaz, this relative of Naomi's husband.

Boaz arrived from the city while she was there. After exchanging greetings with the reapers he said to his foreman, "Hey, who's that girl over there?"

And the foreman replied, "It's that girl from the land of Moab who came back with Naomi. She asked me this morning if she could pick up the grains dropped by the reapers, and she has been at it ever since except for a few minutes' rest over there in the shade."

Boaz went over and talked to her. "Listen, my child," he said to her. "Stay right here with us to glean; don't think of going to any other fields. Stay right behind my women workers; I have warned the young men not to bother you; when you are thirsty, go and help yourself to the water."

She thanked him warmly. "How can you be so kind to me?" she asked. "You must know I am only a foreigner."

"Yes, I know," Boaz replied, "and I also know about all the love and kindness you have shown your mother-in-law since the death of your husband, and how you left your father and mother in your own land and have come here to live among strangers. . . . Bless you for it."

"Oh, thank you, sir," she replied. "You are so good to me. . . ."

One day Naomi said to Ruth, "My dear, isn't it time that I try to find a husband for you, and get you happily married again? The man I'm thinking of is Boaz! He has been so kind to us, and is a close relative. I happen to know that he will be winnowing barley tonight out on the threshing-floor, but don't let him see you until he has finished supper. . . . He will tell you what to do concerning marriage."

And Ruth replied, "All right. I'll do whatever you say."

So she went down to the threshing-floor that night and followed her mother-in-law's instructions. After Boaz had finished a good meal, he lay down very contentedly beside a heap of grain and went to sleep. . . . Suddenly, around midnight, he wakened and sat up, startled. There was a woman lying at his feet!

"Who are you?" he demanded.

"It's I, sir—Ruth," she replied. "Make me your wife according to God's law, for you are my close relative."

"Thank God for a girl like you!" he exclaimed. "For you are being even kinder to Naomi now than before. Naturally you'd prefer a younger man, even though poor. But you have put aside your personal desires. Now don't worry about a thing, my child; I'll handle all the details, for everyone knows what a wonderful person you are. . . ."

So Boaz married Ruth.

I Will Never Leave You

Riders of the Purple Sage
Zane Grey

For a long minute Venters gazed. Then he stretched forth a hand to feel if the gold was real.

"*Gold!*" he almost shouted. "Bess, there are hundreds— thousands of dollars' worth here!"

He leaned over to her, and put his hand, strong and clenching now, on hers.

"Is there more where this came from?" he whispered.

"Plenty of it, all the way up the stream to the cliff. You know I've often washed for gold. Then I've heard the men talk. I think there's no great quantity of gold here, but enough for—for a fortune for *you*."

"That—was—your—secret!"

"Yes. I hate gold. For it makes men mad. I've seen them drunk with joy and dance and fling themselves around. I've seen them curse and rave. I've seen them fight like dogs and roll in the dust. I've seen them kill each other for gold."

"Is that why you hated to tell me?"

"Not—not altogether." Bess lowered her head. "It was because I knew you'd never stay here long after you found gold."

"You were afraid I'd leave you?"

"Yes."

"Listen! . . . You great, simple child! Listen. . . . You sweet, wonderful, wild, blue-eyed girl! I was tortured by my secret. It was that I knew we—*we* must leave the valley. We can't stay here much longer. I couldn't think how we'd get away—out of the country—or how we'd live, if we ever got out. I'm a beggar. That's why I kept my secret. I'm poor. It takes money to make a way beyond Sterling. We couldn't ride horses or burros or walk forever. So while I knew we must go, I was distracted over how to go and what to do. Now! We've gold! Once beyond Sterling, we'll be safe from rustlers. We've no others to fear.

"Oh! Listen! Bess!" Venters now heard his voice ringing high and sweet, and he felt Bess's cold hands in his crushing grasp as she leaned toward him pale, breathless. "This is how much I'd leave you! You made me live again! I'll take you away—far away from this wild country. You'll begin a new life. You'll be happy. You shall see cities, ships, people. You shall have anything your heart craves. All the shame and sorrow of life shall be forgotten—as if they had never been. This is how much I'd leave you here alone—you sad-eyed girl. I love you! Didn't you know it? How could you fail to know it? I love you! I'm free! I'm a man—a man you've made—no more beggar! . . . Kiss me! This is how much I'd leave you here alone—you beautiful, strange, unhappy girl. But I'll make you happy. What— what do I care for—your past! I love you! I'll take you home to Illinois—to my mother. Then I'll take you to far places. I'll make up all you've lost. Oh, I know you love me—knew it before you told me. And it changed my life. And you'll go with me, not as my companion as you are here, nor my sister, but, Bess, darling! . . . As *my wife*!"

Until Two Hearts Are One

If ever two were one, then surely we,
If ever man were lov'd by wife, then thee.
If ever wife was happy in a man,
Compare with me, ye woman, if you can.

—Anne Bradstreet

More than shy kisses or sweet moonlit walks, love that leads to lifelong commitment makes the earth to tremble and the angels in heaven to sing. With such a declaration, two lovers become one. Questions about the future fade, and a deeper love alights.

The opportunities for romance are just beginning. No longer simply nibbling at courtship's delights, the lovers are beckoned to feast on true love, to invite its growth, and to put their faith into making it last forever.

The Most Beautiful Bride

Anne's House of Dreams
L. M. Montgomery

But it was a happy and beautiful bride who came down the old, homespun-carpeted stairs that September noon—the first bride of Green Gables, slender and shining-eyed, in the mist of her maiden veil, with her arms full of roses. Gilbert, waiting for her in the hall below, looked up at her with adoring eyes. She was his at last, this evasive, long-sought Anne, won after years of patient waiting. It was to him she was coming in the sweet surrender of the bride. Was he worthy of her? Could he make her as happy as he hoped? If he failed her—if he could not measure up to her standard of manhood—then, as she held out her hand, their eyes met and all doubt was swept away in a glad certainty. They belonged to each other; and, no matter what life might hold for them, it could never alter that. Their happiness was in each other's keeping and both were unafraid.

You soothe my soul.

You fill it with so tender a sentiment

that it is sweet to live. . . .

—Julie de L' Espinasse

Count the Ways, Please

Pride and Prejudice
Jane Austen

Elizabeth's spirits soon rising to playfulness again, she wanted Mr. Darcy to account for his having ever fallen in love with her. "How could you begin?" she said. "I can comprehend your going on charmingly, when you had once made a beginning; but what could set you off in the first place?"

"I cannot fix on the hour, or the spot, or the look, or the words, which laid the foundation. It is too long ago. I was in the middle before I knew I *had* begun."

"My beauty you had early withstood, and as for my manners—my behaviour to *you* was at least always bordering on the uncivil, and I never spoke to you without rather wishing to give you pain than not. Now, be sincere; did you admire me for my impertinence?"

"For the liveliness of your mind, I did."

"You may as well call it impertinence at once. It was very little less. The fact is, that you were sick of civility, of deference, of officious attention. You were disgusted with the women who were always speaking and looking and thinking for *your* approbation alone. I roused and interested you, because I was so unlike them. Had you not been really amiable, you would have hated me for it; but, in site of the pains you took to disguise yourself, your feelings were always noble and just; and, in your heart, you thoroughly despised the persons who so assiduously courted you. There—I have saved you the trouble of accounting for it; and really, all things considered, I begin to think it perfectly reasonable. To be sure, you know no actual good of me—but nobody thinks of that when they fall in love."

Although all those who

fall in love do so in the same way,

not all fall in love for the same reason.

There is no single quality which is

universally loved.

—José Ortega y Gasset

Love's Royal Arrival

Beverly of Graustark
George Barr McCutceon

"I deceived you for months, Beverly—my Beverly, but it was for the best. In defense of my honor and dignity, however, I must tell you that the princess has known for many days that I am Dantan. I told her the truth when Christobal came that day with the news. It was all well enough for me to pass myself off as a vagabond, but it would have been unpardonable to foist him upon her as the prince."

"And she has known for a week?" cried Beverly in deep chagrin.

"And the whole court has known."

"I alone was blind?"

"As blind as the proverb. Thank God, I won your love as a vagabond. I can treasure it as the richest of my princely possessions. You have not said that you will go to my castle with me, dear."

She leaned forward unsteadily and he took her in his eager arms. Their lips met and their eyes closed in the ecstasy of bliss. After a long time she lifted her lids and her eyes of gray looked solemnly into his dark ones.

"I have much to ask you about, many explanations to demand, sir," she said threateningly.

"By the rose that shields my heart, you shall have the truth," he laughed back at her. "I am still your servant. My enlistment is endless. I shall always serve your highness."

"Your highness!" she murmured reflectively. Then a joyous smile of realization broke over her face. "Isn't it wonderful?"

"Do you think your brothers will let me come to Washington, now?" he asked teasingly.

"It does seem different, doesn't it?" she murmured, with a strange little smile. "You will come for me?"

"To the ends of the earth, your highness."

Married Love Rekindled

The Enchanted April
Elizabeth von Arnim

Now Frederick was not the man to hurt anything if he could help it; besides, he was completely bewildered. Not only was his wife here—here, of all places in the world—but she was clinging to him as she had not clung for years, and murmuring love, and welcoming him.

...What had happened, why she was here, why she was his Rose again, passed his comprehension; and meanwhile, and until such time as he understood, he still could kiss. In fact he could not stop kissing; and it was he now who began to murmur, to say love things in her ear under her hair that smelt so sweet and tickled him just as he remembered it used to tickle him.

And as he held her close to his heart and her arms were soft round his neck, he felt stealing over him a delicious sense of—at first he didn't know what it was, this delicate, pervading warmth, and then he recognized it as security. Yes; security. No need now to be ashamed of his figure, and to make jokes about it so as to forestall other people's and show he didn't mind it; no need now to be ashamed of getting hot going up hills, or to torment himself with pictures of how he probably appeared to beautiful young women—how middle-aged, how absurd in his inability to keep away from them. Rose cared nothing for such things. With her he was safe. To her he was her lover, as he used to be; and she would never notice or mind any of the ignoble changes that getting older had made in him and would go on making more and more.

I confess that I love him—

I rejoice that I love him—

I thank the maker of
       Heaven and Earth—

that gave him me to love—

the exultation floods me.

—Emily Dickinson

A Beauteous Destiny

Beauty and the Beast
retold by Clifton Johnson

As soon as the seven days were past she returned to the castle of the beast, which she reached late in the afternoon. Supper time came and the food was served as usual, but the beast was absent and Beauty was a good deal alarmed. "Oh, I hope nothing has happened to him," she said. "He was so good and considerate."

After waiting a short time she went to look for the beast. She ran hastily through all the apartments of the palace, but the beast was not there. And then in the twilight she hurried out to the garden, and by the borders of a fountain she found the beast lying as if dead.

"Dear, dear Beast," she cried dropping on her knees beside him, "what has happened?" And she leaned over and kissed his hairy cheek.

At once a change came over the beast, and on the grass beside the fountain lay a handsome prince. He opened his eyes and said feebly, "My lady, I thank you. A wicked magician had condemned me to assume the form of an ugly beast until some beautiful maiden consented to kiss me. But I think you are the only maiden in the world kindhearted enough to have had affection for me in the ugly form the magician had given me. When you went away to your father I was so lonely I could no longer eat or amuse myself, and I became so weak that today, when I was walking here in the garden, I fell and could not rise. . . .

". . . Call for help," said the prince. And when she called, several men instantly came to their aid and carried the prince to the palace. Once there, warmth, food, and happiness went far toward restoring him. The next morning he sent for Beauty's father to come and make his home with them, and not long afterward Beauty and the prince were married and they lived with great joy and contentment in their palace ever after.

The Bridal Camp

The Virginian
Owen Wister

"You understood

about this place.

And that's what

makes it—makes

you and me as we

are now—better

than my dreams."

Presently, while they remained without speaking by the pool, came a little wild animal swimming round the rock from above. It had not seen them, nor suspected their presence. They held themselves still, watching its alert head cross through the waves quickly and come down through the pool, and so swim to the other side. There it came out on a small stretch of sand, turned its gray head and its pointed black nose this way and that, never seeing them, and then rolled upon its back in the warm dry sand. After a minute of rolling, it got on its feet again, shook its fur, and trotted away.

The bridegroom husband opened his shy heart deep down.

"I am like that fellow," he said dreamily. "I have often done the same." And stretching slowly his arms and legs, he lay full length upon his back, letting his head rest upon her.

. . . Again he paused and went on, always dreamily. "Often when I have camped here, it has made me want to become the ground, become the water, become the trees, mix with the whole thing. Not know myself from it. Never unmix again. Why is that?" he demanded, looking at her. "What is it? You don't know, nor I don't. I wonder would everybody feel that way here?"

"I think not everybody," she answered.

"No; none except the ones who understand things they can't put words to. But you did!" He put up a hand and touched her softly. "You understood about this place. And that's what makes it—makes you and me as we are now—better than my dreams. And my dreams were pretty good."

He sighed with supreme quiet and happiness, and seemed to stretch his length closer to the earth. And so he lay, and talked to her as he had never talked to any one, not even to himself. Thus she learned secrets of his heart new to her: his visits here, what they were to him, and why he had chosen it for their bridal camp. "What I did not know at all," he said, "was the way a man can be pining for—for this—and never guess what is the matter with him."

Meant to Be

Little Women
Louisa May Alcott

She did not hear him cross the courtyard beyond, nor see him pause in the archway that led from the subterranean path into the garden. He stood a minute, looking at her with new eyes, seeing what no one had ever seen before—the tender side of Amy's character. Everything about her mutely suggested love and sorrow— the blotted letters in her lap, the black ribbon that tied up her hair, the womanly pain and patience in her face; even the little ebony cross at her throat seemed pathetic to Laurie, for he had given it to her, and she wore it as her only ornament. If he had any doubts about the reception she would give him, they were set at rest the minute she looked up and saw him; for, dropping everything, she ran to him, exclaiming in a tone of unmistakable love and longing:

"Oh, Laurie, Laurie, I knew you'd come to me!"

I think everything was said and settled then; for, as they stood together quite silent for a moment, with the dark head bent down protectingly over the light one, Amy felt that no one could comfort and sustain her so well as Laurie, and Laurie decided that Amy was the only woman in the world who could fill Jo's place, and make him happy. He did not tell her so; but she was not disappointed, for both felt the truth, were satisfied, and gladly left the rest to silence.

Love is a great thing,

a great good in every way; it alone

lightens what is heavy, and leads

smoothly over all roughness, for it carries

a burden without being burdened, and

makes every bitter thing sweet and tasty....

Nothing is sweeter than love,

nothing higher, nothing fuller,

nothing better in heaven and earth....

—Thomas à Kempis